The life cycle of a
Chicken

Ruth Thomson

PowerKiDS press.

New York

Published in 2008 by The Rosen Publishing Group, Inc.
29 East 21st Street, New York, NY 10010

Copyright © 2008 Wayland/The Rosen Publishing Group, Inc.

First Edition

Photo credits:Cover main image and 7 Pete Cairns/naturepl.com; cover top right, 13 (top), 23 Jane Burton/naturepl.com; cover middle right, 15 © Royalty-Free/Corbis; cover bottom right, 21 Farkaschovsky/ARCO/naturepl.com; 1, 17, 22, 23 Lukasseck/ARCO/naturepl.com; 2, 20 Jane Burton © Dorling Kindersley/DKImages.com; 4-5 Damschen/ARCO/naturepl.com; 6, 11, 12, 13, 14 Jane Burton/naturepl.com; 8 David Hosking/FLPA; 9 Lynn M Stone/naturepl.com; 10, 23 Foto Natura Catalogue/FLPA; 16 De Meester/ARCO/naturepl.com; 18 Jane Burton/ Corbis.com; 19, 23 Wermter/ARCO/naturepl.com

Library of Congress
Cataloging-in-Publication Data

Thomson, Ruth, 1949-
  Chicken / Ruth Thomson. -- 1st ed.
      p. cm. -- (Learning about life cycles: The life cycle of a chicken)
  Includes index.
  ISBN-13: 978-1-4042-3715-5 (library binding)
  ISBN-10: 1-4042-3715-1 (library binding)
  1. Chickens--Juvenile literature. 2. Chickens--Development--Juvenile literature. I. Title.
  SF487.5.T46 2007
  636.5--dc22
                                    2006033086

Manufactured in China

Contents

Chickens live here 4

What Is a chicken? 6

Laying eggs 8

Keeping eggs warm 10

Hatching 12

Chicks 14

Learning 16

Growing up 18

Pullets and cockerels 20

Adult chickens 22

Chicken life cycle 23

Glossary 24

Index 24

Web Sites 24

Chickens live here

Most chickens live on farms. These chickens roam around outside. They are called free–range. They are fed grain, but also scratch the ground to find seeds, insects, **grubs,** and worms.

What is a chicken?

Chickens live together in a group called a flock. The male is called a cock.

comb

beak

wattles

long tail feathers

claws for scratching

6

The female is called a hen. The cock chooses a hen and dances around her with one wing held out. After they **mate**, the hen will lay some eggs.

Laying eggs

The hen finds a clean, dry, quiet place to make a nest. When she is about to lay an egg, she clucks, fluffs up her feathers, and squats over the nest.

The hen lays one egg each day.
She keeps laying until she has
a **clutch** of seven
to ten eggs.

Keeping the eggs warm

The hen sits on the eggs to keep them warm. She turns them around several times a day to keep them warm all over.

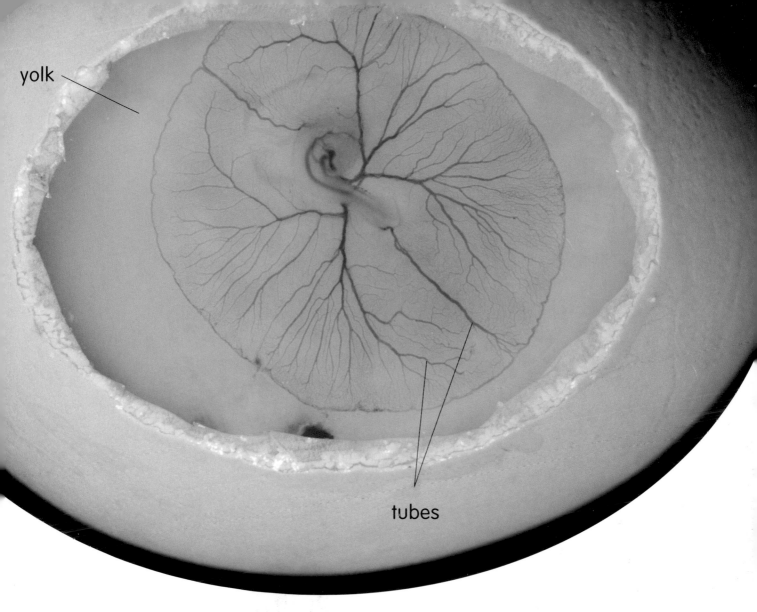

yolk

tubes

A chick begins to grow inside each egg. The egg **yolk** is its food. Air comes through holes in the eggshell. The red tubes carry air and food to the chick.

Hatching

Every day, the chick grows bigger.
After three weeks, it fills the egg.
It has a sharp bump called an
egg tooth on its **beak**.

It taps the eggshell
with its egg tooth
and makes a hole.

It keeps tapping.
The hole
gets bigger.

The eggshell
cracks and breaks
apart and then
the chick **hatches**.

It is wet and tired from
pushing so hard, so it
rests in the egg.

Chicks

The chick stands up and shakes itself dry.
Its body is covered with soft, fluffy **down**.

The hen waits for all the eggs to **hatch**. Then she leads the chicks out of the nest to find food. If a chick loses sight of her, it cheeps loudly.

Learning

The chicks go everywhere with their mother. She shows them how to drink and what is good to eat.

1 day

At night, they hide under her wings to keep warm and safe.

Growing up

The chicks grow bigger and feathers grow on their wings. They still follow their mother around. She shows them where to **roost** and how to avoid danger.

10 weeks

The chicks grow feathers all over. They find their own food now, take **dust baths**, and run around by themselves.

12 weeks

Cockerels and pullets

By now, chickens have a **comb** and **wattles**. Young males are called cockerels.

14 weeks

A young female chicken is called a pullet.

5
months

Adult chickens

Now the chickens are fully grown.
They are able to produce young
of their own.

Chicken life cycle

Eggs
The hen lays a **clutch** of eggs in a nest.

Hatching
The eggs **hatch**.

Adult chickens
Chicks have become grown-up hens and cocks.

Chicks
The chicks learn how to find food.

Glossary

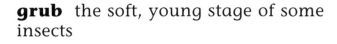

beak the hard part of a bird's mouth

clutch a group of eggs that a hen lays

comb the fleshy, red crown on top of a chicken's head

down the light, soft feathers of chicks

dust bath a chicken's way of cleaning its feathers by flapping around in earth

grub the soft, young stage of some insects

hatch to come out of an egg

mate when a male and female join together to produce young

roost to sleep at night

wattles the two red flaps that hang under a chicken's chin

yolk the yellow food sac for a growing chick inside an egg

Index

Web Sites
Due to the changing nature of Internet links, PowerKids Press has developed an online list of Web sites related to the subject of this book. This site is regularly updated. Please use this link to access this list: www.powerkidslinks.com/llc/chicken/

beak 6, 12

chick 11, 12–13 14–15, 16–17, 18-19, 23
claws 6
clutch 9, 23
cock 6, 7, 23
cockerel 20
comb 6, 20

down 14
dust bath 19

eggs 7, 8–9, 10–11, 12–13, 15, 23
eggshell 11, 12, 13
egg tooth 12

feathers 6, 8, 18–19
flock 6
food 11, 15, 19, 23

hatching 12–13, 15, 23
hen 7, 8–9, 10, 15, 22, 23

nest 8, 15

pullet 21

roost 18

wattles 6, 20
wings 7, 17, 18

yolk 11